THE MEXICAN–AMERICAN EXPERIENCE

COMING TO AMERICA THE MEXICAN-AMERICAN EXPERIENCE

ELIZABETH COONROD MARTINEZ

Coming to America
The Millbrook Press
Brookfield, Connecticut

For my brother and greatest inspiration:
Philip Wayne Coonrod, 1940–1984.

Library of Congress Cataloging-in-Publication Data
Martinez, Elizabeth Coonrod, 1954–
The Mexican-American experience / by Elizabeth Coonrod Martinez.
p.   cm.—(Coming to America)
Summary: Traces the dual heritage of Mexican Americans as
early settlers before the formation of the United States and
as more recent immigrants who came to escape political and
economic turmoil in their homeland.
ISBN 1-56294-515-7
1. Mexican Americans—History—Juvenile literature.   2. Mexican
Americans—Juvenile literature.   [1. Mexican Americans.]
I. Title.   II. Series.
E184.M5M376   1995
973'.046872—dc20   94-19625   CIP   AC

Cover photograph courtesy of Los Angeles Public Library

Photographs courtesy of the Library of Congress: p. 10; Bettmann: pp. 12,
14, 17, 25, 43, 49; Culver Pictures: p. 22, 28, 36–37; University of Texas,
Institute of Texan Cultures: pp. 23, 38; Crocker Art Museum, Sacramento:
p. 31; Los Angeles Public Library: pp. 34, 44, 51; AP/Wide World Photos:
p. 46; Gamma Liaison: p. 57 (Douglas Burrows), 58 (Shahn Kermani).
Map by Joe LeMonnier

Published by The Millbrook Press, Inc.
2 Old New Milford Road, Brookfield, Connecticut 06804

CONTENTS

INTRODUCTION

"The blood of all the world's peoples flows in the veins of Americans," the author Herman Melville wrote more than a century ago. "A vast ingathering from every continent, Americans have shared the common denominator of being, in most instances, either immigrants or the descendants of immigrants."

In our time, no less than in Melville's, the United States is a nation of immigrants. Each year hundreds of thousands of people pull up stakes and come to America, most of them in search of a new home. On the streets of American cities, it is common to hear spoken Polish, Korean, Chinese, Italian, Spanish, and scores of other languages.

Like a great magnet, the United States has drawn those whose lives in other places have been filled with misery. Near-landless peasants of Europe, Latin America, and Asia, oppressed Jews of eastern Europe, and political outcasts from dictatorships all over the world have fled their homelands for the United States. "The people I knew believed that America was the last place in the world where we could find freedom," said a recent refugee from eastern Europe.

Here in America, people have overcome their ethnic differences. This has been true since the very beginning of our national history. "I could point out to you," wrote the French immigrant Michel Guillaume Jean de Crèvecoeur in 1782, "a man whose grandfather was an Englishman, whose wife was Dutch, whose son married a French woman, and whose present four sons have now four wives of different nations."

The story of American immigration has unfortunate chapters as well. The ancestors of African Americans, for instance, came to the United States not bound for freedom, but bound by chains and condemned to the horrors of slavery. Nearly every immigrant has encountered discrimination, prejudice, and, all too frequently, outright violence. Sometimes the laws of the United States supported this discrimination. For a long time, people from Asia were turned away from American shores, and refugees from tyranny were sent back to their homelands.

More than 25 million people living in this country are called Latinos or Hispanics. They come from many different countries in Central and South America, including Mexico.

Some Mexicans lived in New Mexico, Texas, and California before those regions became part of the United States. Some came north looking for refuge during the Mexican Revolution of 1910. Others came to work on farms during and after World War II.

Many of these immigrants thought they would return to their own country in a few years. However, they changed their minds and stayed. Their children have contributed in important ways to American society. Those who came to America in the twentieth century have joined with those who have been here since the Spanish conquest. They are all Mexican Americans.

A DETERMINED PEOPLE

1

Mexico City was one of the most fascinating cities on this continent at the beginning of the twentieth century. It had a university, beautiful parks, museums and theaters, and lots of opportunities for people to start their own businesses. But the government was very unstable. President Porfirio Díaz had been a dictator for thirty years. In 1910 the Mexican people rose up in anger against his government. Díaz was finally removed from office in 1911. This is how the Mexican Revolution began.

A new president took Díaz's place, but he was assassinated in 1913. The next president was pushed out of office a year later. In 1920 another president was murdered, and in 1928 once again a new president was killed. By the 1930s, Mexico had settled into a more peaceful time. But the years between 1910 and 1930 were very difficult for the Mexican people, many of whom were killed. Political leaders often had soldiers shoot people suspected of being on the side of their enemies. Also, people who owned property were killed in order to take away their land.

José Rómulo Munguía was born in Mexico City in 1885. He became an orphan when he was eight years old, and he had to look for a job to support himself. As a teenager he became an apprentice, or trainee, in a print shop. When he was eighteen, he opened his own newspaper printing business. His business was successful, but as he walked through the city or rode the streetcar, he saw soldiers everywhere. Sometimes they invaded his business to inspect what he was printing. He began to worry about his family. Now his own little girl was eight years old, and he wanted her to be safe.

In 1926, Rómulo Munguía decided to move his family north, away from the danger of the revolution. He had heard

that San Antonio, Texas, was a town where many other Mexicans lived. Rómulo Munguía decided to take his wife and three children to live there. With just a few suitcases, they rode coaches and trains for several days, traveling 1,200 miles (1,900 kilometers) north and across the border.

San Antonio was not as big as Mexico City, but it was prosperous. Mexicans who were fleeing the revolution found jobs there. Those who didn't know a trade got work clearing land and digging irrigation canals for new landowners who were moving into Texas from the northern United States. Those who knew carpentry built new buildings, canneries, and food-packing plants for the growing community.

Rómulo Munguía worked, saved money, and soon was able to open his own printing shop again. He had learned English quickly, and now he could do printing jobs in English or Spanish, since half the city spoke one language and half the other. His children learned English in school, but they spoke Spanish in their neighborhood and at home.

After school Rómulo's children worked in his printing shop. When the United States entered World War II in 1941, his sons joined the U.S. Army and went to war. His daughter Elvira helped the war from San Antonio, packaging medical supplies and preparing food for soldiers on leave. One day she met a soldier whose name was George Cisneros. He had grown up in New Mexico and Colorado. His parents were migrant workers, who traveled around Colorado to pick crops. They were born in New Mexico, descended from Spanish settlers who had arrived in northern New Mexico in the 1700s.

After World War II was over, George decided to stay in San Antonio. He and Elvira married and made their home in the Spanish-speaking neighborhood where she had grown up. They had several children, but it was their son Henry who was most interested in his grandfather's printing press.

Henry loved to read. He would spend hours in his grandfather's shop reading everything he could. His grandfather had taught him to read Spanish, and he learned to read English in school. Sometimes his grandfather would take him to the library, where Henry could read about San Antonio's two-hundred-year history. Henry was fascinated that San Antonio was built by the Spaniards, then became Mexican, then Texan, and, finally, part of the United States. He wanted San Antonio to be a very important city in the United States. He decided that he would like to be its mayor.

So Henry studied and made good grades in elementary school and high school, and then he went on to college. He got three college degrees, and finally, in 1981, his dream came true. Henry Cisneros became the first Mexican-American mayor of a large city in the United States. He was glad that he spoke both Spanish and English because he could communicate with more people in San Antonio that way. Henry was mayor of San Antonio for eight years. Then, in 1993, the new president of the United States asked for his help, and Henry Cisneros became secretary of the Department of Housing and Urban Development for President Bill Clinton.

Henry Cisneros became one of the most well-known Mexican Americans in this country. His background was like that of many other Mexican Americans, who had parents descended from Spanish settlers, or whose parents had traveled here from Mexico, like Henry's grandfather. José Rómulo Munguía knew that America offered his children and their children a greater promise of prosperity and freedom than they could have in Mexico. His grandson Henry fulfilled that promise by holding one of the highest posts in the government of the United States.

This is the story of Mexican Americans, some of whom were born in the United States and others whose parents or grandparents came here to start a new and better life.

Henry Cisneros, newly appointed Secretary of the Department of Housing and Urban Development. Flanked by Vice President Al Gore and President Bill Clinton, he introduces his family.

PYRAMIDS, PALACES, AND REVOLUTION

2

Many civilizations have left their mark on Mexico since as early as 1500 B.C. The "classic" civilizations—the ones whose works we see in museums today—thrived between A.D. 250 and 900. The Mayas and Zapotecs built pyramids and huge cities on the Gulf of Mexico coast in the Yucatán and Chiapas and in the southern territory of Oaxaca. The Toltecs conquered the other civilizations during the 900s and established their capital city in the central valley, where Mexico City is found today. By the end of the 1400s, the Aztecs had risen to power. This was the last culture to thrive in Mexico before the Spaniards arrived. The Aztecs were one of seven allied tribes, or groups of people, who spoke the Nahuatl language and had traveled from North America to settle in the lush Mexico City valley. They arrived in the eleventh century, about nine hundred years ago, and within four hundred years they had become the dominant power in Mexico. They built splendid cities, using the technology of previous civilizations, such as the Toltec.

This mural from the temple of Chichén-Itzá shows life in a riverside Mayan settlement sometime between 1200 and 1540.

The Aztecs depended on agriculture, particularly the cultivation of maize (corn). The large valleys between the tall mountains of southern Mexico were ideal places to plant corn and other vegetables and fruits. The Aztecs had a strong military and conquered other tribes in the South and along the Pacific Coast. Then they demanded tribute, or payments of corn and other crops, from them. As the Aztec empire grew, the rulers demanded gold, copper, cotton, and precious stones from the other tribes. Huge caravans of these goods would often arrive at the Aztecs' capital city, Tenochtitlán. They built huge temples in Tenochtitlán, not only for religious purposes but also as homes for their emperors. There were no horses until the Spaniards arrived. All the work of building and making things was done by the slaves captured in their many conquests.

The Arrival of the Spanish ▪ Moctezuma (or Montezuma) was emperor when the Spanish conquistador (conqueror) Hernán Cortés arrived in 1519. Cortés first made friends with tribes along the Gulf of Mexico coast—people who were tired of Aztec rule and wanted to help Cortés overthrow them. Cortés learned a lot from these people before he traveled to Tenochtitlán. He took a woman who spoke several tribal languages with him to serve as his interpreter. The Spaniards called her "La Malinche."

Cortés was lucky, too. The Aztecs believed that members of the earlier Toltec civilization had become gods and would come back someday. Those people had light skin like the Spaniards. The Aztecs also believed the Toltecs would return from the East. So when they saw Cortés and his men on horses, which they had never seen before, they thought the Spaniards were Toltec gods. They welcomed them and gave them gifts. But all along Cortés was plotting to kill the Aztec rulers and take over their land.

A painting by Juan Ortega of Cortés meeting Moctezuma for the first time. Cortés planned from the start to have the Aztec emperor killed.

By the following year Cortés had won many battles. Then he killed Moctezuma. The Aztecs gained one last victory, however, and barricaded themselves in Tenochtitlán. The last of the Aztec emperors was chosen: Cuauhtémoc. He gave orders to defend their city, which the Aztecs did for a long time. But Cortés got stronger as more people from other tribes joined his army. In 1521 the Spaniards drove the Aztecs out of Tenochtitlán and took Cuauhtémoc captive. He was forced to accompany Cortés and his men as they traveled south, conquering additional native peoples. Cortés burned the bottom of Cuauhtémoc's feet, torturing him to reveal where he could find gold. But Cuauhtémoc never told him. Finally, in 1525 the last Aztec ruler, Cuauhtémoc, was killed.

Spanish Rule ▪ The Spanish conquered Mexico, claiming it as a colony of Spain. They named it New Spain and turned Tenochtitlán into their headquarters, which they called Mexico City. The Spaniards built on top of the Aztec ruins and tried to destroy evidence of the previous civilization. They built palaces and churches and in 1551 founded the first university on this continent, in Mexico City.

Priests from the Spanish Catholic Church arrived with Spanish soldiers, and they soon built a cathedral in Mexico City on top of the ruins of the largest Aztec temple. The Spanish continued this habit of building on top of native buildings. But they were never able to cover up Mexico's spectacular past.

Mexico has at least a dozen pyramid sites—more than any country in the world. At each site there are also several large and small temples and other buildings. Some were hidden for many years as the weather chipped away at the buildings and grass grew over them. Some of the pyramids were built as early as the fifth century and are still visible today.

A Busy Colony ▪ During the three hundred years that Spain colonized Mexico, it rebuilt Indian cities to suit its European culture. Silver mines, livery stables, tailor shops, and road-houses for stagecoaches became common. The Spaniards killed many thousands of Indians as they conquered Mexico and moved into Central and South America. They also explored North America all the way to Alaska, but the northern tribes were harder for them to conquer, and the Spaniards had to compete with the French for territory as well.

Mexico City always remained the Spanish headquarters, where the king of Spain established a viceroy, or ruler, in charge of the new continent they had conquered. A palace was built for the viceroy in Mexico City, where everything official in the colony had to be approved.

The Aztecs and all the other Native Americans became the slaves and servants of the Spanish. They built their cities and raised crops for their military and also for the Catholic

Church. Meanwhile, the Spaniards who arrived to live in the colony were given large tracts of land, called land grants. According to Spanish law, their families would inherit these lands, even though they had first belonged to the Indians. Indians were not allowed to own land, except in certain regions.

Many Spaniards married Indians, and their children were the future Mexicans, also called mestizos, meaning of mixed Spanish and Indian heritage. But in Mexico City only pure-blooded Spaniards were allowed to hold high-level positions. Many Indians died from diseases that the Spaniards brought to the continent. In the 1600s the pure Indian population had greatly decreased, and the ruling Spaniards owned most of the lands.

As the cities in Mexico grew, more and more shops were opened that made crafts, clothing, and such things as saddles and metalworks. The Spanish controlled the shops and any work done by the Indians. Anyone who worked—in the cities or on farms—had to pay tribute, or taxes, to the government. Many Indians and mestizos suffered hard times paying taxes out of the little money they made. As the years went by, they became increasingly angry at the Spanish government.

Spaniards and Mexicans looking for better opportunities moved out to the far reaches of the Spanish territory. They settled the frontier in California, New Mexico, and Texas. One of the earliest settlements was in New Mexico, where the city of Santa Fe is found today. The palace for the Spanish governor in Santa Fe, built in 1610, is the oldest building in North America. The Indians expelled the Spanish in 1680, but they were reconquered by the end of the century. The Spanish founded more villages along the Rio Grande (Big River), including Albuquerque, which was settled in 1706. But the Spanish continued to fight the Navajos, Apaches, and Comanches in the area for many years.

In 1709 a priest who was touring the San Antonio River valley in Texas, sent a letter back to Mexico City that described this area as a perfect place for a settlement. In 1714 a Texas governor was named, and thirty families were granted land in what would become the city of San Antonio. The residents of this town were able to fight the local Native American tribes. By the end of the 1700s, immigrants from French Louisiana and also from the new country called the United States were moving into Texas. So Texas was settled by many different Europeans besides the Spanish. In the end, they would fight for control.

New Spain Becomes Mexico ▪ After two hundred years, Spain began to have trouble controlling its colony from so far away. While Spain was busy fighting several wars in Europe during the 1700s, many Spanish rulers in Mexico City became greedy and abused their power. Spain lost a war against France, and was ruled by the French at the beginning of the 1800s. The French Revolution of 1789 caused kings to lose power, while the people became more independent. The idea of independence began to inspire Mexicans who did not want to live under Spanish rule.

As the Spaniards fought the French to regain control of their country in Europe, the Mexicans rebelled and declared their independence in 1810. War broke out, and for eleven years people loyal to the Spanish government fought those who wanted to be independent. In 1821 independence was won, and Mexico became a new, free country, with a territory that bordered Guatemala in the South and touched the borders of Oregon, Kansas, and Louisiana in the North. However, the independent Mexican government had trouble controlling this huge territory. The new government leaders often fought each other for power. Then, far from Mexico City, Americans, who were rapidly settling the region of

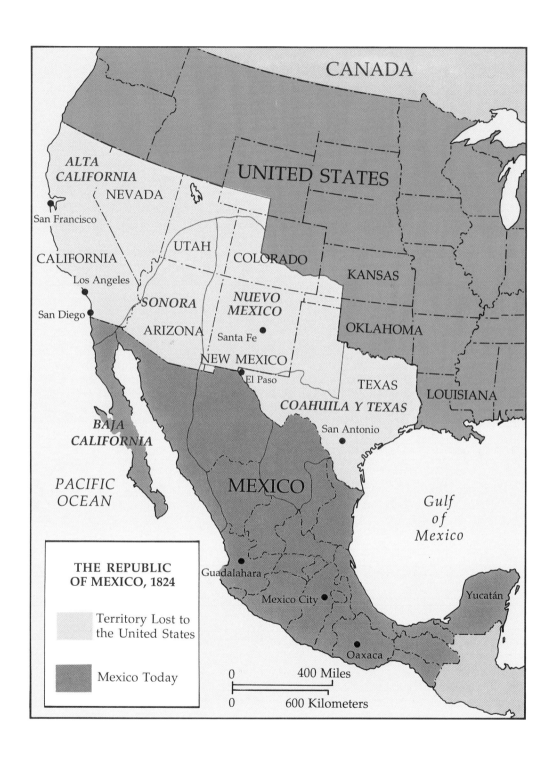

CANADA

UNITED STATES

ALTA CALIFORNIA

NEVADA

San Francisco •

CALIFORNIA

Los Angeles •

San Diego •

UTAH

COLORADO

KANSAS

SONORA

NUEVO MEXICO

ARIZONA

Santa Fe •

OKLAHOMA

NEW MEXICO

El Paso •

TEXAS

LOUISIANA

COAHUILA Y TEXAS

BAJA CALIFORNIA

San Antonio •

PACIFIC OCEAN

MEXICO

Gulf of Mexico

Guadalahara •

Mexico City •

Yucatán

Oaxaca •

THE REPUBLIC OF MEXICO, 1824

Territory Lost to the United States

Mexico Today

0   400 Miles

0   600 Kilometers

THE GRITO DE DOLORES

Right after midnight on September 15, 1810, a priest named Miguel Hidalgo y Costilla climbed to the tower of a church in a small Mexican village called Dolores. He was the leader of a group of mestizos who wanted freedom from Spain. They had planned their revolt for many months, and now the moment had arrived to declare their rebellion against Spain. Father Hidalgo rang the bell to call the villagers to the church, and then he let out a cry from the tower. The people yelled back, "Viva Mexico! (Long live Mexico!)." Then they went out and captured Spanish soldiers and locked them in jail.

Less than a year later, Spanish loyalists captured Hidalgo and shot him. The struggle for independence continued for eleven years. The *Grito de Dolores* (The Cry of Dolores) became the anthem and Hidalgo the father of the movement.

When Mexicans and Mexican Americans gather to celebrate Mexico's independence day, they are honoring Hidalgo. Although the official holiday is September 16, at parties people often shout "Viva Mexico!" at midnight on September 15.

Father Miguel Hidalgo, the first to raise his voice in the Mexican battle for independence from Spain.

Texas, began to demand independence. They were angry when the new government outlawed slavery in 1829. A president elected in 1833, General Antonio López de Santa Anna, gave the territories less power in his central government. That meant that each territory could not make its own laws but had to ask permission in Mexico City. The Texans were outraged. They declared war, and the famous battle was fought at the Alamo, where the Texans were defeated. They fought more battles, and finally beat Santa Anna's troops. Texas became an independent nation in 1836.

Meanwhile, Mexico was also having trouble with California. Although the Spaniards had explored the California coast and frequently took goods from the area by ship, they had never had large settlements because the Indians kept fighting them off. Now Russia and Great Britain were settling along the northern California coast.

"The Surrender of Santa Anna," by William H. Huddle. After this defeat, Mexico lost Texas to the United States.

War With the United States ▪ Mexico's new government had little money, and its military was weak after three decades of fighting. The United States had been a country for sixty-four years and was much stronger. Immigrants from Europe were pouring into the United States and getting more and more interested in Texas and California.

In 1845, nine years after Texas had become an independent nation, the U.S. Congress voted to admit Texas into the United States. Mexico, which had refused to recognize Texas's independence in the first place, broke off diplomatic relations with the United States. In this way, the U.S. annexation of Texas was a major cause of the Mexican War, which broke out in 1846.

Most of the battles of the Mexican War were fought in California, Texas, New Mexico, and Mexico. The Mexican Army was defeated in every battle and finally surrendered in September 1847, when U.S. troops captured Mexico City.

The war ended with the Treaty of Guadalupe Hidalgo on February 2, 1848. Mexico had to cede, or give up, nearly half of its territory—comprising ten present-day states, including California, Nevada, Utah, Colorado, Arizona, New Mexico, and Texas—to the United States. In return, the United States paid Mexico $15 million.

Five years later, in 1853, Mexico sold the United States a 30,000-square-mile (77,700-square-kilometer) strip of land (today's southern New Mexico and Arizona) in a deal called the Gadsden Purchase.

The war with the United States had weakened the Mexican government, which struggled along for a few years until one of its most impressive presidents, Benito Juárez, came to power. Juárez helped stabilize the government and in 1857 brought more freedom to Mexicans by drafting a new constitution. He separated church and state as the United States had done and reduced the power of the Catholic Church.

Benito Juárez, president of Mexico from 1806 until he died in 1872. A Zapotec Indian raised in desperate poverty, he helped Mexico and its people more than any other leader had before.

He also tried to find a way to heal the country's financial problems. But when he suspended payments to foreign countries for their loans, these countries became angry. France, Spain, and Great Britain sent ships to the port of Veracruz in 1861 and demanded payment. The Spanish and British left in 1862 after understanding Mexico's situation, but France continued to fight with Mexico for a year. Finally they occupied Mexico City, and Juárez and members of his government had to flee for their lives. France's ruler, Napoleon III, then sent Maximilian to rule Mexico.

The United States had recognized President Juárez and pressured France for two years to leave Mexico. But the United States was involved in its own Civil War and could not help Mexico. Then the French were pressured in Europe, and in 1867 they finally pulled out their troops. Maximilian stayed and was soon killed by Mexican soldiers.

Juárez was reelected president, and the Mexican government was stable again until he died in 1872. A new president was overthrown by a general, Porfirio Díaz, in 1876. He became a dictator who only helped the rich landowners, adding to their large ranches by giving them land that belonged to Indians. Mexicans who had small properties or worked for wealthy ranchers were cheated by their bosses, taxed by the government, and often killed if they did not obey. These Mexicans and Indians began to look for leaders to help them rebel against Díaz.

The Last War ▪ The Mexican Revolution broke out in 1910. This was the last war the Mexican people suffered. It was during this bloody period that many Mexicans immigrated to a safer place to live—the United States.

The leaders of the revolution forced out the dictator, but they also fought each other for control of the country. Many Mexicans had to change sides or flee for their lives until the revolution was finally over and the country settled down.

Although Mexico has been a stable republic for more than sixty-five years, the Mexican people have not always had enough jobs or received good prices for their crops. They have been heavily taxed and have seen their money lose value year after year.

Some have looked across the border to the United States, the land where their forefathers had lived, and decided to start a new life in the North.

THE CALIFORNIA SETTLERS | 3

The first Spanish ship docked off the California coast in a bay near present-day San Diego in 1542. The Spanish traded with Native Americans and moved on. Other Spanish ships explored the coast in 1602, but it was not until one hundred and fifty years later that colonization began.

Spanish soldiers began building military forts (presidios) between San Diego and San Francisco, and the Catholic priests traveling with them built churches called missions. Only priests and soldiers lived in these first settlements. Since the early 1500s, the Spanish conquistadores were always accompanied by Catholic priests. The priests often documented their explorations for the Spanish court. A Franciscan priest, Father Juan Crespi, wrote the following in his diary when he came upon the coastal valley that would later become Los Angeles:

> Wednesday, August 2, 1769: We entered a very spacious valley, well grown with cottonwoods and alders, among which ran a beautiful river from the northwest.

A priest and his entourage are shown founding the city of Los Angeles. The first Europeans to settle in California were Spanish conquistadores and priests.

Here we felt three consecutive earthquakes in the afternoon and in the night. . . . The plain where the river runs is very extensive. It has good land for planting all kinds of grain and seeds, and the most suitable site for a mission, for it has the requisites for a large settlement. As soon as we arrived about eight [natives] from a good village came out to visit us; they live in this delightful place among the trees on the river. They presented us with some baskets of pinole made from seeds of sage and other grasses. Their chief brought some strings of beads made of shells, and they threw us three handfuls of them. Some of the old men were smoking pipes well made of baked clay and they puffed out three mouthfuls of smoke. We gave them a little tobacco and glass beads, and they went away well pleased.[1]

Twelve years later, forty-four Spanish and mestizo settlers arrived at the settlement known as El Pueblo de la Reyna de Los Angeles, or "The Town of the Queen of the Angels." By 1790, Los Angeles was a busy little town of two hundred people. There were missions and farms in nearby valleys, where people grew maize, grain, beans, lentils, and garbanzos. They also raised cattle and sheep. In the town of Los Angeles, people worked as shoemakers, blacksmiths, weavers, tailors, masons, and servants. They spoke Spanish, although Native Americans who lived in or near the town spoke their own languages. Los Angeles was at the heart of the area within New Spain called Alta California, or Upper California.

Alta California, Mexico ▪ In 1821, when Mexico gained its independence from Spain, Los Angeles' nationality changed from Spanish to Mexican. The people who lived in Los Angeles and other small towns in Alta California started holding elections for their representation in Mexico City. Ships were arriving from South America to trade goods, and other traders came on horseback from Mexico and the United States.

In 1830, Los Angeles' population was 1,180. Some of the residents were foreigners from the nearby United States. About sixty students went to a public school in Los Angeles; other children attended mission schools. More people moved in and businesses opened; Los Angeles was becoming an important city.

As the city grew, its streets were given the names of its prominent citizens, the ones who owned large ranches south of town. Their names—Carrillo, Pico, Sepulveda—are still visible in Los Angeles today. More and more people wanted to live in Alta California, and the U.S. government asked to buy it. The Mexican authorities said no, but they would not be strong enough to back up their position.

California, United States ▪ Because of the Gold Rush, San Francisco and other towns in northern California grew more quickly than Los Angeles did. Mexicans who had large ranches in northern California often were pushed off their land by the immigrants who began arriving in hordes to prospect for gold and settle in this new American frontier. Some Mexicans relocated to the Los Angeles area, but even there they had a difficult time keeping their land.

During and following the Gold Rush, Native Mexicans lost most of their land. They had Spanish land grants, or deeds issued by the Spanish royal court, that declared the land theirs. But the newcomers brought new, United States laws, and Spanish ownership was declared invalid in most cases. Some Mexicans did not have official deeds, and so they could not even fight for their land in court. But the Mexicans who did have a Spanish deed were easily tricked or lied to in court since they could not understand English. Sheriffs came to

In "Fandango" Charles Nahl paints an idyllic picture of joyful Mexicans in a lush California landscape. By the mid-1800s, wealthy Mexican ranchers would be driven from their lands.

move the Mexicans off their land after a judge had given removal orders. If the Mexican ranchers did not leave, they were often killed. Others were pressured into selling portions of their land. When the new owners wanted to buy more of a ranch, they would steal cattle and burn property in order to make the Mexican owner so poor he had to sell off the rest of his ranch.

For many years, Mexicans were killed—often by lynching (or hanging)—when they refused to leave their land. Between 1848 and 1948, the number of Mexican Americans lynched in the Southwest and in California was greater than the number of blacks lynched in the Deep South. Two decades after the United States took over California, the Spanish-speaking Californians had lost their large ranches and most of their wealth to the newcomers.

A Mixed Heritage ▪ Although they lost control in northern California, Mexican Americans still had some political control in Los Angeles. When city elections were held in 1850, Mexicans as well as newcomers were voted into government positions. After the American occupation of California, the population of Los Angeles grew rapidly. So did the number of newspapers. By 1856, Los Angeles had two newspapers: *La Estrella de Los Ángeles* (The Los Angeles Star) was bilingual, and *El Clamor Público* (The Public Clamor) was in Spanish. American newspapers were just getting started, but by 1870 two more Spanish ones were published: *La Crónica* (The Chronicle) and *Las Dos Repúblicas* (The Two Republics). While the majority of the population was no longer Mexican American, the number of Spanish-speakers in Los Angeles remained strong.

Los Angeles was changing rapidly. In 1850 there were 1,610 people living there. By 1860 the population jumped to 4,385. Because numerous English-speaking people moved in, the Mexican population dropped from 75 percent in 1850 to less than 50 percent in 1860.

Racism and violence against Spanish speakers increased with each new wave of arrivals. Some of the Americans who moved into California formed their own communities, separate from the original Mexican residents. Some were bullies and attacked Mexicans just for speaking Spanish. Although criminals could be found among both Anglos (whites) and Mexicans, when a Mexican was caught he was treated worse than an Anglo. Some Anglos would say, "Why don't you go back to Mexico?" But they did not realize that these Mexicans had lived there longer than they had.

In 1877 newspaper editor José Rodríguez complained about the city's plan to tear down Pío Pico's home near the main plaza. Pico was one of the main founders of Los Angeles, and Rodríguez said it was important to preserve his home as a museum. In 1845, Pico's home had been the official capitol and meeting place in southern California. Even so, the Anglo leaders decided to destroy it.

As Mexican Americans lost control of their city, the areas where they lived received fewer public services. Roads remained unpaved; street lamps were not installed. Mexican Americans paid taxes, but their neighborhoods grew poorer while the new parts of Los Angeles were built up.

Since Mexican Americans felt segregated from the growing city, they looked for something to make them feel positive about their heritage. It became more important than ever to celebrate their Mexican victories. Cinco de Mayo, on May 5, and Independence Day, on September 16, were remembered with parades, bands, proud speeches, good food, and dancing.

Boomtown! ▪ The 1880s brought another population boom to Los Angeles. Immigrants from many different countries began pouring into California. This time, however, they were not

34

Mexican-American
students at San Fer-
nando Junior High
School in 1939.

looking for gold. They came because many new industrial jobs were opening up. The construction of the first transcontinental railroad had already brought many workers to the area in the 1860s. Miles of new tracks were constructed in the following decades. Electric streetcars came into use, and gas companies spread at the turn of the century. New businesses sprang up. Italians, Russians, Chinese, and many other immigrant workers were attracted to California. Often they found people of their own heritage who had been living there since the Gold Rush.

By 1910, Los Angeles had become a city of many cultures, but it still had a large population of Mexican Americans. Now new Mexicans immigrated to Los Angeles and other cities in the United States to escape the Mexican Revolution. The new immigrants from Mexico discovered streets named by their ancestors and businesses operated in Spanish by some of the descendants of the founders of Los Angeles. They felt as though they were still at home in Mexico, and they were able to continue speaking Spanish—the strongest link they had to their centuries-old culture.

CINCO DE MAYO

Although some people in the United States assume that May 5 is Mexican independence day, this date is actually a celebration of the Mexican victory over the French. When Napoleon III's troops invaded a weak Mexico in 1862, they landed at the port of Veracruz on the Gulf of Mexico and began a march into Mexico City. Just outside the city, the six thousand French troops met with opposition. Fewer than four thousand Mexicans—some soldiers and many Puebla townsfolk with no military training—fought the well-trained French valiantly. Soon a thousand French soldiers lay dead, and the French were in retreat.

The French attack Puebla. The towns-people's heroic resistance on May 5, although shortlived, is still celebrated today.

The Mexicans used farm implements, rocks, and their own cattle to drive the French back to the coast.

Napoleon was furious and sent 30,000 more soldiers to Mexico, who soon conquered their way to Mexico City and executed many Puebla residents as punishment. The French installed Emperor Maximilian, who ruled Mexico until his execution in 1867.

Mexicans and Mexican Americans remember Cinco de Mayo as a glorious day. It was this first victory against the French that gave them hope to keep fighting for the return of their own Mexican president, Benito Juárez.

THE SOUTHWEST | 4

The region between Texas and California did not have cities that grew as quickly as San Antonio and Los Angeles. However, the Mexican-American people who lived there continued their mestizo tradition long after the U.S. conquest of their lands.

The famous trade route, the Santa Fe Trail, brought many travelers through New Mexico and Arizona on their way to California. In 1850 a man who later married a Mexican-American woman in California kept a diary as he made his way from Missouri. He was fascinated by the people he met and discovered many traditional Mexican foods in the small villages of the Southwest:

> October 19: At Galisteo [near Santa Fe] I made the acquaintance of Don Manuel Baca, whom I found to be very gentlemanly. He speaks English well. . . . Here I ate my first *tortilla* [flat bread made from corn].

> October 22: In Manzana, an Indian village of about one hundred families, abundance reigns, at least of

La Bahia Presidio in Goliad, Texas, was built about 1722.

corn, every house full of it, piles out of doors. . . . Two trains of *carretas* [wagons] freighted with chile passed us on their way from El Paso to the Salinas. . . . The people of La Joya had apples sweet to the taste.

November 13: San Antonio was celebrating the *fiesta* of the patron saint, and the village was in the merriest mood. . . . After partaking of some *miel*, or cornstalk molasses, I slept comfortably. Next morning my host [served me] a dish of stewed mutton, followed by *chile*, with good bread and water.[2]

Native New Mexicans ▪ Many Mexican Americans in northern New Mexico built businesses and large ranches, turning the region into a thriving area by the turn of the century. One such Mexican American was Felix Martínez. He was born in Peñasco near Santa Fe, where he started several businesses. First he had a chain of stores along the railroad track. He then sold these and went into the insurance business in Las Vegas, New Mexico. In 1884, when he was twenty-seven years old, he entered politics. He was a legislator for the territory of New Mexico (which did not become a state until 1912), owned a newspaper, and helped create New Mexico Highlands University as well as a hospital in Las Vegas.

In 1897, at the age of forty, he moved with his wife and seven children to El Paso, Texas, where he started the *El Paso Daily News*. He started several other companies there and also developed an irrigation system in El Paso and nearby Mesilla Valley in New Mexico. He was a very talented man, fluent in both English and Spanish like many other New Mexicans.

Several Mexican Americans were active in politics in New Mexico. They helped the region become an official state after sixty years as a territory. Dennis Chávez was born in 1888 in a town called Los Chávez, near Albuquerque. He had to leave school at the age of thirteen to support his family after the death of his father. But he never stopped studying. Every night after work, Chávez visited the Albuquerque library, studying engineering and American history and politics. Thomas Jefferson was a tremendous influence on him. In 1917 he moved to Washington, D.C., to work as a clerk for a senator while studying at Georgetown University Law School. After receiving his law degree in 1920, he set up a law practice in Albuquerque and soon entered politics himself. As a U.S. senator, he became famous for obtaining free textbooks for public school children. He represented New Mexico in the Senate from 1935 until his death in 1962. President Lyndon B. Johnson gave the eulogy for his funeral.

One Mexican American became the first woman to gain influence in New Mexico politics. Concha Ortíz y Pino grew up in Galisteo on her family's sheep ranch and became a legislator at the age of twenty-five. From 1937 to 1943 she represented New Mexico at home and in Washington, and even in Mexico City. She sponsored a state law that allowed Spanish to be taught in the seventh and eighth grades in New Mexico. She also helped change a law that allowed property to be taken away from people for nonpayment of taxes.

The First Immigrants ▪ While Mexican Americans such as Martínez, Chávez, and Ortíz y Pino were born in New Mexico, other Mexican Americans came to the United States because their lives were in danger during the Mexican Revolution. In fact, about 10 percent of Mexico's population migrated to the United States in the first three decades of the twentieth century. As the United States grew, it needed workers, especially in the Southwest and in California.

Now that train tracks crisscrossed the country, agricultural products could be shipped anywhere, but only if there were enough people to gather the crops quickly. Other workers were needed to can and pack the fruits and vegetables in factories. Other parts of the country wanted the cantaloupes, grapes, lettuce, and citrus fruits that grew in the warm climate of California.

The Newlands Reclamation Act, passed in 1902, inspired the construction of irrigation projects in the Southwest. Desert areas were transformed into fertile lands. Crops of fruits and vegetables were shipped by railroad to the East. From Texas came cotton, which was in great demand in eastern cities.

Mexican immigrants were recruited to work in the fields and in factories. They were happy to find jobs in the United States because the Mexican Revolution had left many of them unemployed in Mexico. American bosses discovered that Mexicans were very good workers. They would work for less money than Americans, too. For many Mexicans, low wages in the United States were still better than the pay they would receive in Mexico, if they could find jobs there at all.

When the revolution finally came to an end in 1935, life became more settled in Mexico. Fewer Mexicans crossed the border during the six years that followed. However, the United States entered World War II in 1941, and many American farmers and workers were drafted into the service. Once again Mexicans were called to the north to work. Job agents, who charged Mexicans a fee for the jobs they got them, traveled by railroad into Mexico to recruit workers for the United States. A special law was passed in 1942, called the Bracero, or temporary worker, program. It allowed U.S. employers to bring Mexicans over the border to work in the fields until the season's crop was in. These laborers were required to return to Mexico at the end of the season.

The Bracero law said that Mexican workers should be housed, fed, and given medical care while they worked for several months on a farm. In reality, the lives of these workers were often very grim. They were picked up at the border and driven, often in overcrowded trucks, to the place they would

There has always been a dark side to the Mexican dream of a better life in the United States. Here, a two-year-old boy looks for food in an empty icebox; his mother cannot find work.

work. They often had to live crammed together in rundown buildings with no heat and only an outhouse for a toilet. They seldom received medical attention. Many became ill or died of heatstroke from working long hours under the hot sun.

The Mexicans suffered, but there were few jobs in Mexico, so some stayed and looked for other kinds of work. Jobs in canneries and meat-packing plants paid better than work in the fields. Women often found jobs cleaning houses or doing laundry, and men found jobs as window washers, gardeners, and floor waxers.

Some Mexican immigrants who arrived as temporary Bracero workers never returned to Mexico. Some of the men married Mexican-American women, and their children were born in the United States. Their children became a new generation of Mexican Americans.

RAMON'S EXPERIENCE

Ramón Gonzáles was born in the state of Guanajuato, Mexico, in August 1922. His father took care of his grandfather's sheep and cattle. When Ramón was only six months old, his father decided to go to the United States where he could get a better job to support his family:

My father took my mother and me to El Paso, and from there we went clear to California. You didn't need to have any papers or anything, you just pay. At the border there was a bridge there and they just paid five centavos. They went to Mendota, California, because it is in the San Joaquín Valley, which is known for cottonpicking. Mendota is a big cotton place. At first when we got there it was pretty hard because they didn't pay much money, they paid 10 cents an hour. . . . My mother used to cook meals for the Mexican workers. We lived in Mendota for about six years. Then we moved from Mendota to San Bernadino; all my relatives lived in San Bernadino. My relatives wrote to my father and told him he could make more money picking oranges than he could on the cotton. So that's how come we moved there. I used to help him picking oranges. I was small but I could pick a little bit and help him. He used to get three cents a box. Then I only helped him on the weekends because I started going to school. There were Mexican kids there but they were all from the city, born in the States. I was the only one born in Mexico.[3]

Migrant workers — men, women, and children — in a bean field during the 1920s.

THE VOICE OF PROTEST | 5

The need for Mexican farmworkers continued after World War II was over. Many Americans left their low-paying jobs on farms for better-paying jobs in factories and big cities. But the Bracero law was no longer in effect. The growers needed farmworkers so badly that they would often pay smugglers to bring them across the border. These smugglers also charged the Mexicans money to hide them from the border guards and take them to a place where they would find work.

The U.S. Immigration Service launched a campaign in 1947 and again in 1954 to get rid of "wetbacks," as Mexicans without documents were called. Wetback is an insulting term. It was first used because some Mexicans swam across the Rio Grande into Texas. This was the only way they had to come here on their own.

In 1952, Congress passed a law that said anyone caught bringing in undocumented people for jobs would be punished. This slowed down the flow across the border, but only for a few years. Meanwhile, the people who had been working on farms all their lives—whether they were Mexicans or Mexi-

A border patrolman arrests illegal Mexican immigrants. After questioning, they will most likely be sent back to Mexico.

can Americans—had received almost no pay raise for decades. Unions were organizing to help workers all over the United States. Mexican Americans, many of whom were desperately poor, would soon have a special leader to protest the terrible conditions in which they worked and lived.

César Chávez ▪ César Chávez was born on a farm in Yuma, Arizona, in 1927. His father's dust-bowl farm failed in the Great Depression of the 1930s, so the family joined other migrant workers in California. As a child, César worked seven days a week alongside his father. The wages they earned were so small that even when the entire family worked they often did not have enough to eat. Sometimes they were not paid at all. The man who hired them would disappear or call the Immigration Service agents to get the workers off his property when the crop was in. César remembered searching for wild mustard greens to eat to keep from starving. He didn't own a pair of shoes until he was fifteen, and he was never able to finish high school. He and his family were American citizens, but they seemed to have no rights at all.

When César was a teenager, he got kicked out of movie houses because he was "Mexican." He joined the U.S. Navy during World War II, where he was treated like a servant. After completing his service, he went back to work in the fields. In 1952 a labor organizer who was helping Mexican Americans recruited César Chávez. During the next decade Chávez learned the techniques and philosophy that helped him establish the National Farm Workers Association (NFWA), an organization to protect workers and improve their lives. A thousand people joined this union in 1962.

In 1965, Chávez's union joined with other unions in a strike that lasted five years. Workers united in nonviolent protest, they refused to labor in the fields, they formed picket lines, and they marched to California's capitol building in

PLANTING AN IDEA

After ten years working for another union, César Chávez decided he wanted to start his own organization to help Mexican-American farmworkers:

In March of 1962 I came to Delano to begin organizing the Valley on my own. I drew a map of all the towns between Arvin and Stockton — 86 of them, including farming camps — and decided to get a small group of people working in each town. For six months I traveled around, planting an idea. We had a little card with space for name, address and how much the worker thought he ought to be paid. We distributed these cards door to door. . . . Some 80,000 cards came back to us. I was shocked at the wages people were asking. The growers were paying $1 and $1.15, and 95 percent of the people thought they should be getting only $1.25. Sometimes people scribbled messages on the cards, like "Do you think we can win?" So I got in my car and went to see those people. The first big meeting of what we decided to call the National Farm Workers Association was held in September 1962, at Fresno, with 287 people.[5]

César Chávez (front left) leads striking grape pickers on a march in Delano, California, 1965. Walter Reuther (to the right of Chávez), president of the powerful United Auto Workers Union, has joined forces with the NFWA.

Sacramento. Nonviolence was the theme of La Huelga (the strike). Chávez practiced the teachings of Mohandas Gandhi and Martin Luther King, Jr., who both said that you can change the way people treat you without turning to violence.

Not until the mid-1970s were contracts signed in which farmworkers received better wages. Farmworkers had earned barely a dollar an hour for decades; with the help of the union they now received two dollars an hour.

After that victory, Chávez dedicated his life to improving working conditions for all farmworkers. He traveled, made speeches, called strikes, and fasted—going without food for weeks at a time—to win attention for his cause. Some people called him a Gandhi of the United States, but Mexican Americans said he was their most wonderful leader since President Benito Juárez.

By the 1970s many factories had expanded and were on the lookout for cheap labor. The economy was booming, and border guards let Mexicans cross because they knew that employers needed more workers.

People in the United States protested. Some said that Mexicans were taking their jobs away, and they wanted them to go home. Others said that Mexicans had been encouraged to come and that they helped the U.S. economy. Meanwhile, in Mexico almost no jobs were available outside Mexico City and Guadalajara. Many more Mexicans decided to come to the States because they had heard about the possibilities here.

Living Together With Difference ▪ People who were upset about the number of undocumented Mexicans in this country often treated Mexican Americans as though they had no right to live here either. Their names sounded the same, and they spoke Spanish, and sometimes they did the same kinds of jobs. However, they were born in the United States, and sometimes their parents and grandparents had been born here, too.

A young Mexican-American performer celebrates Mexico's independence day in 1940s Los Angeles. An American flag and a banner with the words "Grito de Dolores" are symbols of her dual heritage.

Some people tried to force Mexican Americans to speak only English.

Graciela Olivárez was born in a small mining town near Phoenix, Arizona. She didn't like to go to school, because the teachers got mad at her for speaking Spanish.

She wrote:

> In school in the Southwest you are literally punished physically if you are caught speaking Spanish in the hallways. The argument was that you couldn't learn English if you spoke Spanish. You were taught that you mustn't speak Spanish, yet you went home and your parents said you must speak Spanish because the Mexican heritage is rich.[4]

After high school Olivárez found a job at a Spanish-speaking radio station in Phoenix. She enjoyed talking in Spanish and English on the radio and playing Mexican music. She was also worried about the rights of Mexican Americans, so she got involved in the civil rights movement of the 1960s. Then her work impressed the president of the Notre Dame Law School. He invited her to go to law school. She did and became the first woman to graduate from the Notre Dame Law School, in 1970. Then, in 1977, President Jimmy Carter gave her an important job researching population growth.

Graciela Olivárez was a professor at the University of New Mexico Law School during the late 1970s, and in 1980 she opened Albuquerque's first Spanish-language television station. Her station was connected to Univision, the company that began Spanish television in the United States. Olivárez believed strongly that Mexican Americans have a right to keep their language and their culture, which should not prevent them from being successful Americans.

A BETTER
WORLD

6

Since illegal immigrants continued to cross the border from Mexico in large numbers, the U.S. Congress passed a new immigration law in 1986. It included amnesty. That meant that anyone who had lived in the United States for more than five consecutive years could apply for citizenship. The approval process took three years. Thousands of people did this (not just Mexicans) and became new citizens in 1989. The law said that people who did not show their citizen identification card, or a birth certificate if they were born in this country, would not be able to get a job.

By the late 1980s the number of jobs decreased in the United States. Often there were more farmworkers than jobs picking crops. Factories began laying off rather than hiring. Some people complained that they could not get jobs because Mexican immigrants were getting them. Even some Mexican Americans complained about Mexicans.

Several members of Congress with the support of President George Bush and later of President Bill Clinton decided to help Mexico create more of its own jobs. In 1993 the U.S. Congress approved the North American Free Trade Agreement. Called NAFTA, this agreement will gradually eliminate tariffs and other trade barriers between the United States, Canada, and Mexico.

Many American and Mexican leaders hoped that NAFTA would stem the flow of Mexicans across the border. They also hoped that the economies of both the United States and Mexico would improve through a more open trade relationship between the two countries.

A Common Story ▪ Many Mexican Americans hope people in the United States will understand their own history better. Whether they recently became citizens or their great-grandparents lived here before the land belonged to the United States, Mexican Americans are Americans. Many are still treated as though they are not citizens of the United States. Here's an example:

In 1992, Martha Alicia Vázquez was driving her beat-up Volvo station wagon along a lonely stretch of road between Las Cruces and Deming, in southern New Mexico. These two towns were only about a two-hour drive from the Mexican border. Vázquez was a lawyer in Santa Fe, the capital of New Mexico, who had driven south to look for a family member of someone she was defending in court.

Suddenly, a green U.S. Border Patrol van was driving quickly behind her and flashing its lights. Vázquez stopped her car and sat in it trembling. She wished she had brought someone with her. The Border Patrol agent walked all the way around her car twice and stooped to look inside before he spoke. Vázquez knew she had not done anything wrong, but her heart was pounding. She remembered how it had felt when she was a little girl in Santa Barbara, California, where her parents and other berry pickers feared the green vans.

Vázquez was completely fluent in English. However, when the Border Patrol officer asked her a question in English, she answered him in Spanish because she was nervous. After looking at her documents, the officer let her leave. For some people, Vázquez thought, it was not so easy.

This is how some Mexican Americans live their lives. The fear felt by parents and grandparents never goes away. It is passed on to the children, just as it was to Vázquez, who was born in California. She was a graduate of Notre Dame Law School and a respected lawyer in Santa Fe. In 1993 she became a federal court judge. Vázquez was also a wife, the mother of four children, a Girl Scout Leader, and a volunteer Spanish teacher. She was used to working several jobs, just as her parents had.

Vázquez's mother was born in Dallas, Texas, but grew up in the big city of Guadalajara in Mexico. When her mother was a teenager, she moved with her mother to California, where they picked avocados and packed them in crates. Vázquez's father, who was born in Mexico, came to California in the 1950s to pick crops. Several times he was arrested by the men in the green Immigration vans and deported—that is, delivered back across the border into Mexico. But he kept returning because he could not find work in Mexico.

After he married Vázquez's mother, he was able to become a U.S. citizen. When their daughter Martha Alicia was born in 1953 in Santa Barbara, they decided to move to Guadalajara where they had relatives. But when Martha Alicia was five, her parents returned to Santa Barbara and never left again.

She went to school and learned English quickly. She helped her parents learn English so they could get better jobs than picking crops. When they did, they bought a house in Santa Barbara, and Martha Alicia attended a private Catholic school. Martha Alicia received such good grades in school that she won a scholarship to go to college. She also worked at a grocery store while she went to high school to save money for college.[6]

Martha Alicia Vázquez's story is like that of many Mexican Americans. They work hard for a good education and become productive members of their communities. Some are lawyers and judges, like Vázquez. Others are political leaders. Among these are Gloria Molina, who has been a Los Angeles county supervisor for many years; Federico Peña, mayor of Denver for several years; and Henry Cisneros, former mayor of San Antonio.

Other Mexican Americans are outstanding teachers or school principals. Some, such as Edward James Olmos, are actors. Others write novels and stories or study science and become astronauts, such as Ellen Ochoa and Sid Gutiérrez. These Mexican Americans also continue to speak and write in Spanish, the language that they inherited from the Spaniards who first conquered this continent. They also enjoy Mexican traditions, such as celebrating Cinco de Mayo, and eating foods that their Native American forefathers made from maize and chile.

The New Generation ▪ Sometimes the new generation of Mexican Americans does not learn to speak Spanish because of pressure to speak English in their American communities. Many are very serious about getting college degrees. Others, however, who grow up in big cities such as Los Angeles and Chicago, face many problems as do many inner-city kids. Drugs, crime, and violence are a part of their daily lives.

Creating a better future is a great challenge for these kids. They face a world filled with prejudice and racism. But there are many Mexican-American leaders and role models who try to help young people get out of their difficult living conditions. These leaders talk to young people at neighborhood

56

Mexican-American children growing up in Los Angeles face a world filled with poverty and violence.

gatherings, at weddings and funerals, and at celebrations of Mexican holidays.

Mexicans are not the only Spanish-speaking immigrants to the United States. Starting in the 1970s, many people from Central and South America have come to live in the United States. They have fled from danger and war in their countries or they have come to look for jobs. Sometimes people confuse them with Mexican Americans.

Most immigrants are poor when they arrive here, and they don't speak English. They are young and healthy, though. They get jobs, support their families, and help their children receive an education so that they can have choices in life. This has been true for many Mexican Americans.

The Mexican-American actor Anthony Quinn said that when he was a little boy he had a strong imagination, which helped him to see his future. His father died when Anthony was nine, and he grew up during the Depression, when it was impossible to afford an education. He worked on an apricot ranch as a teenager, then as a ditch digger, and later as a butcher and a salesman. Each time he figured out how to do the job after he had convinced his employer that he knew how to do it. His father had been an actor, and Quinn figured out how to act in the same way as he learned how to do any other job. Through the years, he has made about 120 movies. He is one of the most respected Mexican-American actors in the country today. When he was a little boy, Quinn said, "I imagined a better world than I'd found. I had illusions about what the world should be, a kind of beauty that I had not experienced yet."[7]

Anthony Quinn made the world a better place for him and for Mexican Americans. He invites Mexican-American children to use their imaginations to discover what kind of world they want to live in. If they work and get an education, they, too, can become a famous actor, an astronaut, a teacher, or whatever else they want to be.

Children in traditional Mexican costumes on Cinco de Mayo, a celebration of courage and hope.

NOTES

1. From a Herbert E. Bolton 1916 text, *An Illustrated History of Mexican Los Angeles, 1781–1985* (Los Angeles: University of California Chicano Studies Research Center Publications, 1986), p. 21.

2. From Marjorie Tisdale Wolcott (1929), *Pioneer Notes* (New York: Arno Press, 1976), pp. 23, 25–27, 32–33.

3. From John J. Poggie, Jr., *Between Two Cultures* (Tucson: University of Arizona Press, 1973), pp. 10–12.

4. From Al Martínez, *Rising Voices* (New York: Signet Books, 1974), p. 133.

5. From Edward W. Ludwig, *The Chicanos: Mexican American Voices* (Baltimore: Penguin Books, 1971), pp. 105–106.

6. From "A Most Unusual Judge," *The Albuquerque Journal*, Sunday *Sage Magazine*, June 6, 1993.

7. From Al Martínez, *Rising Voices* (New York: Signet Books, 1974), p. 147.

MORE ABOUT MEXICAN AMERICANS

Atkin, S. Beth, *Voices from the Fields: America's Migrant Children.* New York: Little, Brown, and Co., 1993.

Bandon, Alexandra. *Mexican Americans.* New York: Macmillan Childrens Group, 1993.

Brimmer, Larry D. *A Migrant Family.* New York: Lerner, 1992.

Catalano, Julie. *Mexican Americans.* New York: Chelsea House Publishers, 1988.

Cedeño, Maria, E. *César Chávez: Labor Leader.* Brookfield, Conn.: The Millbrook Press, 1993.

De Varona, Frank. *Miguel Hidalgo y Costilla: Father of Mexican Independence.* Brookfield, Conn.: The Millbrook Press, 1993.

Krull, Kathleen. *The Other Side: How Kids Live in a California Latino Neighborhood.* New York: Dutton Childrens Books, 1994.

Marquez, Nancy, and Theresa Perez. *Portraits of Mexican Americans.* Carthage, Ill.: Good Apple, 1991.

Martinez, Elizabeth, C. *Henry Cisneros: Mexican-American Leader.* Brookfield, Conn.: The Millbrook Press, 1993.

Rodriguez, Consuelo. *César Chávez.* New York: Chelsea House Publishers, 1991.

INDEX

ABOUT THE AUTHOR

Elizabeth Coonrod Martinez grew up in Mexico and moved to the United States at the age of seventeen.

She was a journalist before turning to teaching at the University of New Mexico, where she also studies Spanish literature.

She has translated several works from Spanish to English and written biographies of Henry Cisneros and Edward James Olmos.

She lives in Albuquerque, New Mexico.